an important note fi

hi. there are two ways y

1. whenever your heart ˪ ˻ ˻ you to, pick up this book,
    flip to a random page and let the universe give you
    the poem you need most. do not read in order. do
    not read in one go. do not read unless something
    inside of you is begging to.

2. read it like a story, front to back, with as few
    breaks as possible. visualise each poem as a
    different chapter in a love story, because you
    should know that it is exactly that. read it like you
    are me, you are heartbroken, you are in love. read
    it and let yourself feel it; all of it.

you will not find a single capital letter in this book,
mainly because i do not believe in the idea that any one
letter should hold more weight than the next. i must
give a trigger warning for some of the poems in this
book; my poetry is built from my life, everything is
real, everything is me, some of it is not very pretty.
there will be talk of eating disorders, sexual assault,
body image, mental health and suicide. i sincerely
apologise to anyone who this may trigger, please take
the time to look after yourself.

the last thing i will say to you before you leave me to
flip to the next page, is that this book, much like the
world, deserves your voice. so, do not be shy. immerse
yourself in it; read it out loud, on top of mountains or
hidden away in bedroom closets. share it with everyone
or no one.
whisper it.
scream it.
read it,
and try to enjoy every single moment of it.

contents

before

the fall

after

to the girl i used to be,
to the girl i became,
to the girl i will be.
i will love every single version of us
regardless.

always.

how
sunflowers
bloom under
moonlight

illustrations by frances hammond
isbn: 978-1-3999-1714-8

before

waiting for them

there is just so much to me that i am waiting for
someone to ask about.
no one has yet.
i don't know when someone will,
but i know i will try to wait patiently for them.

for those who love when not yet healed

i think hurt people attract other hurt people.
it's like some sick sixth sense.
we seek each other out,
create a relationship based on anxiety and past trauma
where we race to escape unscathed;
revolving around each other
as if we are each other's suns.
some of us are yet to be healed,
the wounds are still bleeding, scabbing,
not quite faded scars.
i suppose it could be worse though,
imagine an unhealed person finding a healed one,
imagine breaking someone who was so whole
before you.
tearing them apart
the same way
someone once did
to you.

words i do not have the courage to say out loud

i have come to understand that i will always be *a little bit broken.*

i will always have these scars,
and this heaviness around my heart.
i cannot outlive days where i feel like dying,
or outrun moments that leave my lungs empty.
i have been damaged to a point where i no longer remember
being

i n t a c t .

and you can see it in my eyes,
if you look amongst the clutter of blue and green glass,
you can see how i am always on the verge of breaking,
too fragile for my own good.

i am *barely* together most days.

desperate to be happy

i am desperate to be happy again.

it has been so long,
i do not remember what it is that i am chasing.
i do not remember what happiness feels like,

but i know i want it again.
i want it so badly.

homes for the stars

i want to make love like how
the stars find their homes in the sky.

like how:
one twinkling never diminishes the second.
no ones brightness takes away from another's.
i want sex
to be for the both of us,
that i can enjoy it just as much as you can
and that there is no need for darkness between us.

stars,
only stop being stars for three reasons:

1
they collide with a black hole.
they become nothing,
consumed in tidal disruption
by something so much more careless and powerful
than themselves.

2
they collide with another star, quickly.
and at once, both of these stars destroy each other.
a 'romeo and juliet'-esque fate,
they leave nothing behind,
but the reminder that they were once there
to anyone who saw them implode.

3
they collide with another star once again,
but this time,
slowly.
these stars envelop each other,
embracing with caution.
they become one.

a mass of hot, blue brightness,
you see there's beauty in their togetherness.
they way they leave whatever they were before
to join to be something better.

and so i want to make love like how
the stars find their homes in the sky.
slowly.

eighteen reasons i am afraid to marry a woman someday

1
women.
2
wedding cake toppers.
3
wedding cakes in general.
4
venues.
5
more specifically, churches.
6
wondering if i'm wearing too much make up for a
lesbian.
7
being called
a lesbian
and losing my identity as a bisexual woman.
8
the idea that my family who make offensive
gay jokes in private,
will use their attendance at my wedding as means
to prove
they are not
homophobic.
9
the question
'so who's going to wear the wedding dress?'
10
wearing a wedding dress.
11
what if i want to wear a suit?
12
what is she wants to wear a suit?
13

i am afraid
that marrying a women means i can no longer be
attracted to men.
i am afraid i will invalidate my sexuality to an extent
that no one will believe me when i say,
'i also like men.'
14
i have gaslighted myself into thinking
that perhaps i have had it wrong all along.
15
i do not know how to function
if i am not with a man.
16
i seek male validation in an attempt to love myself
and i will not be able to do this anymore.
17
what if i am happier with a woman than i am with a
man?
18
what if i am not?
18
wondering if referring to her as my partner
and not my wife
will upset her.
18
but i am hoping that she will understand how
uncomfortable it is
for my tongue to hit my teeth
and how my jaw freezes up every time
i see the look in someones eyes after admitting
my sexuality.
18
that my phase was never really a phase.
18
that my mum will never truly apologise for telling me
my sexuality was 'just another thing i did for effect
and shock factor.'
18

the fact that my mum thinks my sexuality
is for shock factor.
18
wedding cake toppers.
wedding cakes.
churches.
venues.
my family's perception of me.
18
i am afraid i will lose myself when i find myself with
another woman.
18
the age i was when i first referred to myself as bisexual.
the 18 year old version of me being so disappointed,
that she had the courage to come out so i could live my
life as me
and not under some facade of a straight girl,
but current me does not have the courage to live as
anything else.
18
i am afraid, full stop.
i am afraid of marriage and love and women and life
and how other people will judge me.
18
and women.

oh how i've disappointed myself

i suspect younger me would be disappointed.
i watched the adults in my life ruin themselves,
and i swore i wouldn't turn out like they did.
i wouldn't let my fingers smell of lingering cigarettes
and sadness.
i wouldn't find comfort in staying with someone just
for the sake of it.
i wouldn't drink till i can't remember spilling unkind
thoughts from my intoxicated brain to my mouth.
i didn't want to become someone who couldn't
remember what happiness felt like.

i had promised myself
that i wouldn't stop experiencing sun kissed
evenings where i worshipped the wind,
i wouldn't stop big bellied laughs,
and bright beaming smiles.
i wouldn't stop running from silly boys who were
trying to kiss me in the playground.
i was so much better than that.
i didn't ever want to stop my love for participating in
life.

i think slowly i've been ruining myself.

and i hate it

you know i try so hard to be happy,
to pretend to everyone else that i am.
i fake this self love bullshit time and
time again,
but it's not true.
it never is.

i still hate myself
and my body
and the way my face looks right after i wake up,
when it's all puffy and slightly too red.

i hate my voice
and the way it's always a little bit too nasally.
i hate the way my body feels when i touch it
and so i try not to.
i shower with sponges because it means i don't have to
feel my own hands on my skin.

i hate the way my hair never quite looks right,
it's always messy but never in that 'effortlessly waved'
kind of way,
but more in the 'i spent the whole night tossing and
turning because i'm too anxious to sleep' way.

i hate the distance between my eyes,
and i hate that my eyes are never the sort of colour
people can fall in love with.

i hate my stomach
and my cellulite
and my veins
and my fat rolls
and i hate how whenever i say that i hate these things
everyone goes

'what??? no!!! you're so perfect,
i so wish i had your body!'
no you don't.

no you don't.
and i hate it.

the only way to describe my depression

i can feel this sadness
all over.
it creeps into my bones like a cold, dull ache,
sours my mouth with its metallic taste
and rings in my ears
like an alarm i can never properly silence.
i am infected by it,
i am consumed.

epidemic

somewhere in the world,
there is a girl
being carried out of a club
by a man
she just met.

a man
who approached her while was dancing with friends,
told her
she was pretty,
put his uninvited hand on the small of her back,

and shoved a drink into her mouth.
and she has been conditioned to know that a drink is
currency for her body,
she owes him now, in turn he now thinks he owns her.
and as he carries her out,

while he's fist bumped by other men,
praised for collecting his barely conscious sex doll
for the night,
her head slumps,
her arms limpen,

her eyesight darkens.
she will not remember what happens next,
but there are bruises beginning to form
from his fingerprints,
like her flesh is a fruit too sweet, it is rotting,

they will let her know that this pain will remain long
past the physical does.
the claw marks on the inside of her thighs,
handprints on her breasts,
blood staining her pants.

the first thing she will do the second she gets home is
shower him off of her.
she will let the water run over her, too afraid
of her own body to touch it, she will scrub herself raw
with sponges in a bid to remove his stench.

and when police ask her why she did not report
the sex immediately,
everyone listening will say
'hmm, what a good question.'
not a single person will stop and ask 'why,

the fuck are they calling that sex?'

this man,
this rapist,
will shrug,
he will point out
her underwear choice,

how she touched his arm,
bit her bottom lip,
he will tell everyone
how she wanted it.
she gave him the eye.

and a man in the jury
will listen
and nod.
the defence lawyer will nod.
the world watching the news at home will nod.

this is an epidemic.

this disease is
widespread,
it is infecting your daughters
it will infect your granddaughters.

it is rampant.

somewhere in the world,
a girl
has to live in the prison
her rapist created while
he manages
to walk
free.

97%.
only 4% is ever reported.

is anyone stupid enough to wonder why?

love is a scary thing

i wonder if it is
possible for me to love if i
was never taught how to?

now that i think about it,
i expect it is,
if i could just work through the fear.

but i am too afraid to love,
to be unreasonably vulnerable,
with an emotion i do not know how to possess.

finding someone to fix

some days i wish i was too afraid to love,
but i am not.
i could have my heart broken a million times over
and yet i'd still find a piece to give away to someone.
and if they were broken,
well i'd pick up every shard,
cut my hands bloody in the process,
and i'd put them back together.
and like all the times before,
they'd hand me back that little piece of me that i gave them,
them,
a little bit more broken,
and i'd find someone else to give it to,
someone else to fix.

self projected, self sexualised

you know what no one ever fucking talks about?
the fact that most people never love themselves until
there's someone else is loving them.
to hate every inch of your body until
there is someone else
touching it,
kissing it,
and telling you how attractive they find you.

and i think about this a lot,
how we base our whole self worth on another person's
perception of us.
i mean, fuck,
most days
the only beauty we find in ourselves
is when someone else is inside of us.
how fucked up it all is
that you never love yourself
until someone else is desiring you.

how my illness comforted me

i don't even starve myself properly anymore.
i hang sheets over my mirrors,
i don't weigh my pasta when i'm cooking,
i haven't even weighed myself in months.
i am trying to swallow my eating disorder
but it is stuck in my throat.
i am trying to recover
i am trying so hard
and i feel like such a failure.
it was so much easier to be sick.

squeezed hearts

i have met many people
who have told me
how their ex broke their heart.
how they were
mistreated by them, buried by them
how their ex destroyed their idea of love.

but you know what i haven't heard?
someone telling me about how they broke
someone else.
how they
were the ex that shattered expectations and
ruined their relations.
how they were the villain in their own story.

and this is not a coincidence.
i have not only met good people,
i have met story tellers
who place themselves as the heroes,
the strong ones
for surviving such difficult breakups,
there is never really such thing as love without
one person coming out unscathed,
one of us
had to.
it's just easier to pretend we are a victim rather than
an assailant.

and i don't blame you.
we've all done it.
but if i asked you
to tell me about the person who's heart you broke,
the one you just thought about,
the one you know you damaged.
who you toyed with, emptily promised futures with.
the one you made love you without intentions

of loving back,
would you tell me why you did it?
can you swallow your pride deep enough to spit the
truth back into my hands?

you know i can predict what you'll say.
the cycle of being broken too many times has turned
into being too afraid to love again,

it has turned into
'i have to hurt them before they hurt me because
someone
must leave this relationship with heart ache, right?'

it has turned into
'if i let it happen again,
i will not be able to cope this time.
i cannot watch myself be torn down into another shell
of myself,
there is only so many times i can grow back into me'

it has turned into
'no one will ever be like them,
or hold me like them,
or kiss me like them,
or ruin me like them.
no one
will break my heart like them'

because you told yourself that,
didn't you, love?

you told yourself you wouldn't experience
that sort of suffering again.
in turn, in your own selfish self preservation,
in anticipation,
you did it to someone else.

oh.

but you aren't the villain, not in your story,
no,
you leave that bit out.
in theirs though, that person who was nothing like
the one before,
the one who probably only hurt you
because of *their* ex that broke *their* heart,
in their story, my darling,
you are nothing short of a thief.
i hope that taking their heart and squeezing
it in your hands
made your own feel more full.

because if it didn't,
ah,
well then we are a generation with empty hearts
of others in our hands,
too afraid to let go.

and nobody desires that.

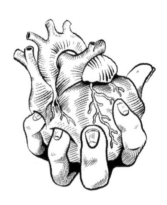

to be normal

i'll admit it.
i day-dream about what it would be like to be normal.

to wake up,
and not dread walking past the mirror for fear of being
sucked in.
i cannot stop the scrutiny once i lock eyes with
whatever *this* is in front of me.
on days when i cannot remember yesterday,
if i wake and see sheets draped over mirrors,
i know i must be kinder to myself today.
i always leave them up.

to open the curtains and instead of
the sun giving me a headache,
it makes me smile.
it has been so long since the sun has seen my teeth.

to eat breakfast,
and i mean properly eat.
not 20 grams of porridge oats made with water,
or a green tea with a slice of lemon on the side,
but real food,
without guilt.
i cannot explain how much jealousy my heart holds for
those who
do not know
the calories in every mouthful they swallow.

to have a place in this world and be so sure that
not only do you fit perfectly,
but the world fits you too.
it has been so long, truly,
since i have felt
like i belong.

their scales tip

i have heard so many unhappy people say that they do
not actually want to die,
that they want the opposite:
to live.

they are just so sick of how mundane
and repetitive their days are that the 'death' they crave
is not one from a skeleton in a cloak, carrying a scythe,

but the sun
after an eternity of clouds,
the breaking
of their chains,
the warmth
of another's body,
instead of
the absence of heat they are so unfortunately used to.

they want to feel something,
after so long of feeling nothing.

i wonder if people who commit suicide want this also,
perhaps they just place the unknowing of life after
death above the life we live now.
i think it says a lot,
that their scales tip towards
oblivion,
rather than
living.

words

and you know words mean everything to me.
most nights, instead of sleeping
i carve myself out of them,
pull words out of my day and build with them.
i have created skyscrapers that tower over us,
bridges some architects would hold envy for
and forests deep enough to hide in.
i do tend to love people who like to hide.
and people who don't hold the same appreciation for
words.
perhaps,
now that i am reflecting,
i suppose i have been expecting too much from those
who cannot understand how in awe
i am,
of the way they can mix letters.

comforter

i relish
in the feeling of being my favourite person's
comfort blanket.
i think i try take their pain as my own,
unintentionally, of course.
i collect their waves of sadness until i feel like i am
about to drown in my man-made ocean.
i bottle their depression,
engulf their eating disorder,
i write their suicide note in my handwriting.

but this is not a mutual agreement,
i cannot give away my emotions as they would theirs.
i do not feel very much of
anything,
anymore.
and so i steal their emotions as my own, pretending
it's some selfless act of self sacrifice,

i don't even mean to do it.

i
just
can't
help
myself.

i want

i want someone to chase after me.

i want my movie scene in the pouring rain,

i want sunflowers because they're my favourite.

i want someone to show up at my house unannounced,

i want hands held in public,

i want to be brought home to meet the parents.

i want a cup of tea in the morning.

i want the love letters,

i want songs sung together,

i want to sit on a beach and watch the sun setting,

i want star gazing.

i want to be missed when we've spent too long apart,

i want nights in together,

i want nights out together,

i want planned futures.

i want playful fights over whose eye colour our babies will have.

i want pictures of us laughing,

i want the last slice of toast because it's always my favourite,

i want the right side of the bed.

i want 'i love you's' traced on my back while i'm half asleep,

i want poems written about me,

i want someone to not be able to take their eyes off of me in a crowd.

i want goodbye kisses
on my forehead,

i want to be made
to feel special.

i just want someone to fucking love me.

i have done all of this,
all of it.

for once,
for once i just want it back.

i am so sick of not being loved.

tracing scars

whenever i have been given somebodies' heart,
i cannot help but trace their scars of previous lovers,
comparing their marks
to my own,
trying to ease insecurities that i will not live up to their
last.

i think one day i might find a heart
with matching scars to my own.
perhaps they will have also traced bumpy scars with
their fingertips,
a braille spelling out everything
they are not.
maybe
we can trace scars together.

beauty

for a while, i had thought beauty was something you
can see, and feel.
it was visible, real, easy to spot.
i thought it was people's faces that held
the most beauty,
with time,
i've begun to learn that we are so much more.
i see it in the souls of strangers,
the way their eyes twinkle when they talk about
something they love,
the way their heart breaks,
the standards they hold themselves to,
the kindness they show others.

beautiful people do not have perfect skin
or perfect hair, perfect bodies.
they have an unruly fire inside of them,
impulsivity mixed with carefulness,
a light that can brighten the day of anyone who needs
their day brightened.
you cannot measure these things, they cannot be born
from nothing,
beauty just is.
it is pure and personal.
it is everything and nothing all at once.

beauty is yours to decide what it is,
and yours alone.

tarmac

i always seem to want what i don't have.
there's this stupid need for something new
deep
in my body
that never seems to be satisfied.

i do not think i will ever be content with the hand
i am dealt,
that there will ever be a time i decide
what i have is enough,
and that the grass
is not always greener.

perhaps

i do not want grass at all,
but tarmac.

a poem for the only two people in my life who are truly in love

i know you have both heard of how zeus split humans
in two.
how powerful they were,
and how he feared them.
soulmates,
he created the search for a soulmate.
together,
you are the personification of that mythology.

you fit so well,
wrapped up together with years of memories,
roots intertwined,
fused by personal growth,
you ground each other. you've built each other.

and alone,
oh god, alone you are just as powerful,
you do not need each other to exist beautifully,
but when you are together,
there is this explosion of technicolor. it is mesmerising.

one of you holds the kindest heart i have ever met
and the other intelligence unmatched.
an unruly determination for life,
and a calmness the ocean would be jealous of.
you both draw breath in rhythm,
hold each other with nothing but respect,
long for each other, with pureness and pleasantness.

one day, if i am so lucky,
i hope to experience a love like yours
and i hope to watch what you already have
flourish.

kinder to me

i really think this is it.
i don't know how much more i can take before

breaking
point.

something
has got to give.

because i am tearing myself apart,
i am causing myself so much pain.

i really wish i was kinder to me.
i think i'm slowly killing my own soul.

self destruct

and there i am,
having one of worst days i've had in a while,
and i find myself in the shower,
absentmindedly turning up the water to the
hottest setting.
i'm standing under the onslaught of heat, watching my
skin get redder
and redder,
eyes closed, fists clenched,
i mean i'm proud of myself for getting into the shower
at all on a day like that.
i'm not proud that burning myself made me feel better.

and then the other day,
oh god,
this day was bad too,
right after my breakup and all i wanted was to be held.
and so i drank,
and drank,
top 5 drunkest i've ever been,
and i let strangers touch me and kiss me.
i didn't even know their names.
i didn't care, i just needed to be needed again.

and then last week,
after i'd spent the entire weekend at some random boys
house,
playing 'perfect girlfriend' and feeling so far from it,
and meeting his parents and his best friends,
i was driving home and i thought
'fuck this.'
i went 120 and i almost crashed twice. and it made
my heart
beat
again.
it felt like i finally took that deep breath i'd been

holding out for.
i loved it.

you see,
this is self destructing bullshit,
its never quite anything that's going to kill me, even if
i wish it would.
i'm so numb most of the time
so desperate to mean something to people i don't give a
fuck about
feel something real and not have to fake smile for once
do something, anything that's going to give me just a
little bit of gratification.
no one really gets it.
this isn't what most people think about when you
mention self harming
but i think most of the things i do to myself hold so
much harm.

i'm so sick of this shit.

purpose

we dance up rainclouds,
bask in the sun,
adorn ourselves with metals and stones.
we close our eyes to songs that make our spines tingle,
read stories of other worlds in a bid to escape our own,
taste a stranger's lips,
let hands intertwine to feel less lonely.
hell, we let bodies intertwine to feel like we are worth
something.
we try to view it all from a different angle,
because i guess the world does look
a hell of a lot different
from underneath someone else.

all of us are searching for some sort of reason to feel
full.
something that'll keep the cogs turning
and our bodies moving.
something that'll make us get out of bed
in the mornings
and open the curtains.
something to think about as we fall asleep.
something that even on our worst days,
gives us just a little bit of purpose.

i suppose that's what this is all about,
all any of us are trying to do is fill ourselves up.
find things that make our mundane days
less
mundane.

suffocation

we are a generation of lonely people in rooms,
toocrowdedtoocrowdedtoocrowded
to breathe.

i am afraid to catch my own breath most days.

safe with me

the night after i sent the boy i live with
to the hospital because he begged me to let him
kill himself,
i ordered us pizza.

6 hours prior
i had been hysterically crying
on the phone to the police in secret.
when they told me they were sending two
cars immediately, i ran to find him,
and i held him while he collapsed into my lap.

he sobbed like he wished his body
would melt into mine and so,
when he told me not to let go,
i didn't.

when the police and paramedics knocked on the door
i whispered in his ear
'please.
please don't hate me.'

the betrayal in his eyes as they walked in has been
burned so deep into my brain,
i cannot forget it.

so this pizza,
was my peace offering i guess.
some stupid,
'i'm sorry i didn't let you do it.'
because truthfully,
i really did feel so guilty.

two weeks later our roles had swapped
and he was holding me up.
i wasn't strong enough to stand on my own.

it was sheer luck we found each other.
some cosmic gift from the universe,
who knew we couldn't live on this earth
alone
anymore.

we are two young
and stupid
kids begging for a place in this world.
we are clinging to anything,
and anyone,
who makes feel something other than numb.

and a few days later,
as he falls asleep in my arms,
head on my chest,
limbs wrapped around my body,
he told me my bed is the only place he feels
safe enough to sleep.

i placed one hand on the top of his head
and told him
he will always be safe with me.

what i so desperately want

i just want someone to look at me,
and know that i am the one.
i want them to tell their mum about me,
all smiles
and giddy.
i want them to hold me high
and i want to feel safe in their arms.

i do not want to be dropped again,
i don't think my body can take another fall.

all i want,
is to belong to someone,
i want it so badly.
to have an undeniable connection that frustrates
everyone around us
because they wish they had what we have.

this isn't flowers on valentines, or proposals on knees,
this is a brush of a thumb on my palm when we're in a
crowded room.
this is a push of hair off of my face and behind my ear.
this is a look
of pure love where no words ever need to be said.
i can give this to someone,
i know that,
but i do not think there is anyone who can give me this
back.

secretly i worry the problem lies with me,
that my expectations are just too high.
i cannot deal with someone else giving me just half,
i need it all.
i need all of them.

for the sake of holding me

can you just
hold me.
just
hold me for the sake of holding me.
not to have sex with me,
not to see me undress,
not so that i end up on my knees.
just hold me.
and kiss me on the top of my head,
brush your thumb over my cheek,
tuck a strand of hair behind my ear.
be gentle, be tender, be humane.
touch me with pure intentions,
kiss me because you like the way my brain works,
or because you think my soul is kind like yours.

i have become so used to being used,
i have forgotten what
love is without sex,
what eye contact is without being on top of
one another,
what wrapping another body around your own without
letting them
inside of you
is like.

i am desperate to experience something real,
something that does not leave me begging for more.
i want to be held.
i want someone hold me,
to cradle me.
be clement in their love for me.
to gaze at me, intently.

i have no room for men who act like wolves anymore.

the place for hungry eyes and clawing hands was never
owned by me,
i had no say in the 'lad culture' that deemed my body
fuckable.
i had no say over who fucked my body,
period.

so hold me,
please.
understand my flinches, understand how i recoil when
you move too quickly.
hold me the way your heart holds patience
and hold me,
for the sake of holding me.

an open letter to the person i hope to fall in love with some day.

hi.

we haven't met yet,
but
i cant stop thinking about you.

i have imagined your laugh in every volume,
every possible tone
and i think my ears could already pick you out of a
crowded room.

i have already named the entirety of our family,
granted,
most of them are dogs,

and i may be open to hearing
some your suggestions,
but i think you'll like most of mine.

sometimes, when i am drifting off into a place where
my subconscious has already met you,
i can picture you laying next to me,

and i swear i can almost feel the heat of your breath on
the back of my neck,
your hair tickling my cheek.

i know you will look at me with only kindness and
warmth in your eyes
and touch me with fingers that are nothing less than
gentle.

i promise to only do the same to you.

let me be happy

if happiness is reliant on another human being
then it makes sense that i am not happy alone.
i wish i was strong enough to be.
i really wish i could be one of those girls
who are content without someone else
but i am not.
and i am longing for happiness.

to be in love with someone is one thing.

to fall in love with them,
is a completely different thing entirely.

and then i fell.

the fall

he saw her

he looked at her,
and it was a look like any other they shared,
stolen from across the room.
filled with want
and hesitation.

but *this one*,
in
this one
he really saw her.
the way her nose sloped into pools of freckles
and sun spots.
how her hair curled around the face
he adored from a distance.
eyes brightened, lips full,
chin tilted up.

god,
she was everything to him.

he likes flowers

there's something so beautiful about falling for
someone new.
learning their intricacies,
and figuring out the way their brain works,
what makes them
tick.
you can't help but compare them to your last,
and almost always you'll believe that this new person
is better.
they'll have a softer voice,
more life in their eyes when they stare at you,
possess a kindness you didn't know was possible
and maybe they'll place their hands on parts of your
body the last person
never touched,
the sweet spots on the side of your waist
that gives you butterflies.
maybe he likes flowers,
or maybe he writes poetry too.
you try not to compare
but you do,
and it makes you like this new person all the more.

he's not you

and then i read my poetry to him.
and he wasn't *you*.
and it was different this time,
it was received with more appreciation,
in a way i had always hoped *you* would.
and he can talk to me
and i mean
really talk,
about anything and everything
and the world, and philosophy and books
and he gets me.
he really, *really* gets me.
with every conversation we have,
i learn a little bit more about him, and every new piece
of information makes me giddy.
and he isn't *you,*
not even a little bit,
he's *him.*

smitten

'smitten,'
he said,
'i told my friends i'm smitten.'

the other night,
as i called him half asleep,
he asked to read to me.
some stupid book
about penguins and i couldn't tell you a word he said,
but i could explain so vividly how
the vibrations of his voice
soothed my soul.
how i slept
more soundly that night
than any other i ever have.
he calms me in
a way i didn't think
was possible.

and i wrote him a card last week
for no particular reason.
i covered both inside pages and
my words accidentally spilt onto the back as well.
he told me
the second he got home
he put it in his current book as a bookmark,
read it 3 times that night before bed
and boasted
to anyone who would listen about
the girl who wrote him a card
just
because.

he calls me beautiful at every chance he gets,
i tell him
i love how

his eyes light up
when he talks about his biggest passions.
he reminds me to eat
and makes sure i always get home safe.
i invite him to dinner with my best friend
in the hopes that
she will love him
just as much as i do.

'smitten?' i asked him,
'i'm besotted.'

greyness

you say that
this city,
is undeserving of me.
that,
i am
uncontainable,
in the life i am currently living.

and i watched you
rattle off compliment,
after compliment,
a declaration
of your
'almost love'

i hear you say things
i have been praying for someone to say about me.
i've never felt
so seen before.
and i really mean it when i say,
not a single word
is ever
out of place.

somehow
even when you're teary eyed,
heart in my hands,
mouth furiously moving,
you still say
everything
perfectly.

and as i watched
our eyes synchronise
in their sadness,
i thought about how you loved

the speckles
of yellow
in mine
and how i loved
the greyness
of yours.

you think your eyes are boring,
but i think they are approachable,
and kind,
and calming.
grey
does not equal
dull,
for me,
grey is a colour
i want to stare
into.

how
appropriate it
all is
really.
my eyes
are exciting
and different
and you think
the world of
them.
yours,
yours are not out of this world,
no,
instead, they hold a stillness
that this world
rarely sees.

i like grey.

a long distance exchange of hearts

perhaps
it was his fault i did not realise i was in love with him.
he made me forget about everything else when we were
together,
so how could i have known?

it was only when we said goodbye,
so sweet
as i relished in this new discovery that my heart now
belonged to him,
and so bitter,
as i knew it would be a long time before i got to see
them both again.

off with him, she went
but in exchange,
i had his.

forehead kisses

'physical touch,' i say,
'is my love language.'
and he asks me,
'what is mine?'

one thing you quickly learn in relationships is
that love,
is not giving as you wish to receive,
but giving what you know they require.

the exchange
of
love
languages.

he shows me his love for me by touch,
even though it is not the way he experiences love.
kisses
on the forehead,

he knows i
go weak at the knees for forehead kisses.
he cringes,
though,

when he sees other couples behave in this way.
he watches,
beady eyed, to make sure no one is watching us, afraid
of the judgement.

so when he kisses me anyway,
he shows me
just how much he loves me
by fighting this fear.

i told him once

that he makes me melt
when he does this,
that i appreciate

every hand hold,
every arm around my side,
every
forehead kiss

so much more,
because i know what each means to him.
he does this,
to make me happy.

he does this,
to try to speak
in a language he is
far from fluent in.

'yours,'
i say,
'yours
is giving.'

my favourite part

my favourite part about being in love
is not loving him,
it is him loving me.
and knowing that, in his eyes,
there is not
a
single
thing
he would change about me.

always yours

and i love you
i do
and i dont know why because
you are so
goddamn
annoying
but i do.
i think always will.

perhaps, i am lovable

he really does make me so content.
when i'm with him,
i don't feel so broken.
and it's not that he's fixed me,
he hasn't,
but somehow he makes me forget that my heart
is bandaged.
he makes me feel lovable.
he's the first man to ever do that.

and he does it with second nature,
this ease that makes me unreasonably angry.
if it was this simple, why was it always so complicated
before him?
why did i always feel
so
unlovable?

with him,
i am so much more than just my body.
i am the fiery light behind my eyes,
the sweet words that drip off my tongue,
the complexity that exists in my head,
i am the essence
of what it is to be
someone he can love.

for some boys,
for some i am just fuckable,
i recognise this now,
but for him, for that man,
oh,
i am
so
much
more.

nicknames

he gave me a nickname.
i've never had one of those before.
he always smiles when he says it.
i can't help but smile too.

i have one for him, in my head.
i daren't say it out loud yet,
but i always smile when i think it.

the imperfect moments

we've had our movie moments,
the ones you replay to help you fall asleep,
the ones that make you feel all tingly,
and warm inside.
and don't get me wrong,
these moments are great,
they're perfect and so long sought after,
but i think i prefer the imperfect moments all the more.
when i can't stop laughing while he's trying to kiss me
and it's all teeth and smiles.
when he's distracting me while i'm driving and i hit
that damn curb,
when he snores in his sleep.
and he can only fall asleep in one specific position,
all curled up on his front, arm underneath himself, face
all squished into the pillow.
somehow he still always looks so peaceful.

i love that one.

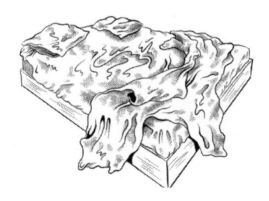

my person

i wrote him a letter once,
right at the beginning of our relationship,
and in it i tried explaining what i meant when i said
i thought he could be
my person.
looking back, god i was naive.
i don't think back then i fully understood what love was
and yet here
i am,
pouring my heart out to this boy
with a smile that makes my insides leap
and a laugh that i feel deep in my bones,
the sort of comforting warmth of happiness.
i never feel cold when i'm around him.

and i keep every single thing that could possibly
remind me of him.
plane tickets, arcade game tokens, cards.
i wonder if he evens knows
that he's the reason i like cards,
i had a burning hatred for them until i'd met him.
but
my person
gave me these,
so now i reread every word as if it's the first time,
and in the sentences where he calls me
his person,
i feel my heart swell with this
overwhelming endearment.
pure delight and elation,
to know not only does understand my phrase,
but he uses it,
towards me.

love languages

i fell in love with you without touching your skin
or without you touching mine.
i fell in love with your words,
and the way you look at me
and the way you make my heart leap.
and i didn't need touch.

oh god,
look at what you've done to me.

skin

the ripples of water can look like skin if you're far
enough away.
all crinkled and moving the way only skin can.

how do i know this?

i used to take a lot of planes, and spend a lot of time
gazing out of tiny oval windows
imagining his skin.
sometimes
i could almost see his scars in that water
and if i just looked hard enough,
deep enough,
i could see my skin with his.
entangled together,
wrapped up in uninterrupted blue.

together.

my throat has forgotten how to

no one ever explained to me
how difficult it is
to look the only person you love in the eyes and tell
them
you have not eaten today.
to see their smile fall, and the look of disappointment
on their face,
in those moments,
i wish the ground would just
swallow me up,
which is ironic, i guess,
because if you think about it,
i haven't swallowed anything solid in three days,
and at this point
i think my throat has
forgotten how to.

locked eyes

i wish i could see
myself in the light

you see me in.
in split second glances,

or moments of real
smiles and loud laughter.

in sleep filled gazes
as i lay on your

chest. and when locked
eyes cant seem to

notice the world around
us. i wish i

could see myself in
the light i see you in.

80

i ask him
if he knows the calories in an average sized apple.
he looks at me,
like i am crazy.

'why,' he asks,
'would anyone know that?'

and i cannot help but chuckle,
that the body he loves to kiss and caress is built upon
knowing
not only the calories in an apple,
but a pear.
half a banana,
3 grapes,
a singular piece of spearmint gum,
a green tea brewed for exactly 4 minutes.

the calculator in my head is exhausting me
with its second nature and its accuracy.
and in some super fucked up, sick way,
i cannot help but feel
proud.

you know i used to love the smell of fresh fruit,
i'd let my nose be engulfed by the scent.
it is only now, i realise that
smelling
is not the same as
eating.
my stomach, empty.
i can feel the jealousy
it holds for my nose
with every grumble
and gurgle.
it is begging to be fed,

always.

this is my existence.
this is all
i have ever
known.

'why,' he asks,
'do you know that?'
and again i chuckle,
i am so glad
that he does not
understand.

he loves me

it is an odd feeling to experience love when you do not
love yourself.

to hear someone list all of the things about you that
make them happy
and know the exact same features
are the ones that keep you up at night,
and make you cry uncontrollably.
they keep you from eating the next day,
and the day after that.

it does not matter how many times i hear him say
i am beautiful,
or how he wouldn't change a thing about me,
i still scroll through the internet looking for
plastic surgeons near me,
or for dieting tips,
home workouts,
ways to get rid of hip dips,
how many calories a cold shower burns,
the best exercises for a thigh gap,
what laxatives
are the most effective.

this is a world i cannot let him know i live in.

part of me wonders, if he truly does love my curves like
he says he does,
or if he would poke fun at my fat
the second we broke up.
i worry that i will become a running joke between him
and his friends as soon as i leave.
i worry,
that i already am.

but i do have days,

i have days where he convinces me.
and on these days, we lay in bed together,
and he kisses every inch of my body while telling me
how perfect i am.
i feel helpless to his love,
and so i surrender myself,
feeling weak and giddy.
for a few moments, i believe every word out
of his mouth
silently praying that this feeling,

won't ever leave me.

but it does.

i go back to the self-loathing, and the starving, and the
scrolling.
my phone's search history is
starting to look like a hell of a lot similar
to how it used to,
those days
i thought i had moved on from, and healed from.
i am beginning to wonder if i ever did,
or maybe
i just got so good at reassuring him i was over it,
i managed to convince myself.

he will not stop telling me he loves all of me.
when i tell him i do not believe him, he says
it only gives him all the more reason to say it.
he will not give up until i agree with him, and even
then, i do not trust that he would stop.
you know, i should be grateful,
and yet i can't help but overflow with this
unreasonable rage that
somehow
he manages to love me,
and i cannot.

the idea of losing you

i am so petrified
of losing you away.

i think i am more petrified
that, actually,
it will be my own doing.

fuckable, not lovable

i really do
self-sabotage
and i end up pushing everyone i love away,
because truthfully,
i just cannot show them how broken i am.
i do not want the pity stares,
or the tight hugs that scream: 'i know you need this.'
'i know you need me.'

i feel simultaneously
like i am too much and too little for him.
i feel it
in my instantaneous replies,
when his take hours at a time.
i feel it
in the way i always wait for him to tell me
he loves me first.
i feel it
consistently,
and constantly.

when i say that i am fuckable, not lovable,
it is not to say i am only desirable for sex.
believe me,
i know my body is not the sort of body boys beg to
have sex with. it is to say
i do not think i am someone who anyone can truly love.
i am too much work,
too difficult,
too complex.

i can feel myself
waiting for him to realise this,
to throw in the towel and tell me,

'you're just too much to deal with.'

the day you leave me

often,
i think about
how i cannot know which time will be the last
that you tell me you love me.
until it is too late.

if only i could know in advance,
i could memorise the way the words feel as they drip
off your tongue and into my ear.
and i could tell you
how you saved me.
how i so deeply love you for it.

but there are some things you cannot plan for,
or predict.
i do not have a crystal ball, and even if i did,
i doubt i hold the willpower to
take my eyes
off of yours
for long enough to gaze into it.

and so i am left in this limbo,
caught between
wanting to never stop hearing how you love me and
hoping you will never say it again
for fear of
becoming too dependent on this medicine, i
will soon
no longer have a prescription.for.

truthfully,
i am petrified of the day you leave.
you do not know what the hole you pulled me out of
looks like,
and if it is of any condolence,
i can reassure you

that it was not my deepest, or my darkest.

but i have this feeling of absolute dread in the pit of my
stomach that tells me,
the next time i trip,
the drop before i hit the bottom will be
longer than any of my others.
and the climb out,
excruciating.

blanket

sometimes i wish
that i had never told you i
write poems.
i think i write about you far too often,
a comfort blanket
i should have long grown out of

and yet,
every night,
i fall asleep cocooned
in a cotton
that feels like
you.

i love him?

i am sure
i love him.

what else could this be?

it is unlike any infatuation i have felt before.
i have never gotten lost
in someone's eyes the way i
have with his.

i swear to you,
i have memorised every golden speckle,
every shade of green,
even the ones that only show up when sunlight
brightens his face.

i must love him.
maybe the issue
is not if, but how.
maybe,
i love him too much

perhaps what i am really questioning
is not if i love him at all
but if i am worthy of love.

yes

if my body is the only reason i am
touched,
caressed,
kissed,
then it is only right that i am loved for my body.
it is, understandable,
that i give it to him willingly.

that i serve myself like a piece of meat.
tied up in ridiculous string,
dowsed with red wine,
i heard
the acidity brings out the flavour,
as if alcohol will make it
easier for me to forget what is happening
and
easier for him to
seduce me.

but,
it is willingly,
right?
i said
yes
to him once, to begin our lives together,
i-
i cannot suddenly start saying
no,
can i?

conditions of love

the downside
to being loved
unconditionally,
is that your conditions
become all the more
visible.

how our love will consume me

someone asked me a question about you today.
they said:
'do you love him as much as you did
when you first met?'

now,
i sat and thought about it for a while,
and i don't.
i don't love you the way i did in the beginning,
all puppy dog eyes
and
hearts in mouths,
and
butterflies,
and
tingly feelings
and
fireworks.

my love for you
is no longer that impulsive rush of desire,
hot headed
and
heavy hearted.

i used to think true love was like a ball of light,
forever glowing and always there,
just effortlessly beaming.
i have begun to learn
that it is more like a bonfire.
in its own way, just as pleasing,
if not more,
but with the added danger,
and its constant need to be fed.

it is hard work,

ensuring our love does not dwindle,
or burn out.
it is even harder work when the feeding
is so one sided.

i do not love you as much as i did in the beginning,
because when your love faded,
i was forced to grow mine.

how unfair this all is,
that now i'm stuck with all of these feelings,
trying to compensate for the lack of yours.

and i think this love,
this bonfire of love,
will eventually consume me.
and it will use me
as its
kindling.

you do not make me feel like i am enough.

i think i would've realised this a long time ago
if i had figured out
just how much i was worth,

if i had realised that
i am more than deserving of the demands
you find too clingy,
or too intense.

i am not
'a psycho'
for being insecure. it was supposed to be
your job
to make sure i felt
invincible.

you cannot label me
and then blame me
for your shortcomings.

what he does not like

sometimes,
i wonder what he does like about me.
i get so fixated
on the back handed remarks,
or the looks he gives me
that say all of the words
better left
unsaid.

there seems to be so much to me
that he does not like

and he does not let me forget it.

oh.

i guess this is it.
i had been so desperate to fall in love,
i don't think i ever took a second to think about what
comes next.
what comes after the love leaves?
i've fallen so far,
i think i've finally hit
rock
bottom.

oh.

after

i thought i had it

i thought i had it.
i thought i fucking had it.
the love and the future and the person,
my person.
i fucking had it for a second there, i really did
and now i've lost it.
oh god,
i've really lost it.

the worst part

the worst part of all this,
the bit i can't think about for too long without my
vision becoming blurry,
or without salty rivers running down my cheeks,
is that while i'm tearing myself apart over you,
i have no idea if you're doing the same for me.
i don't know if you still love me,
or want me.
i don't even know if you're still thinking about me.
you are the only thought i
have had in weeks, months.
i hurt so much for you,
so fucking much,
and i have no idea if you
do the same for me.

i have to move on

i don't want to be with someone who doesn't love me,
who doesn't have this burning need in their chest
to tell me
just how much they do
at every goodbye,
at every hello,
and at every moment in between.
you cannot say it without mumbling, or looking away,
or without me saying it first.
fuck,
i mean,
why are you even with me if you don't love me?
i just want you to feel what i feel,
but you don't,
so i cannot love you anymore,
i just-
i have to move on.

we both always held such a love for bodies of
water.

   yours:
oceans, beaches, lakes.
places where you felt small but significant,
in a way you often did not.
a vastness so mesmerising,
i think you felt at home surrounded by
something so dangerous.

   and mine:
puddles, single droplets of rain,
small streams in forests.
i liked the way they were so often overlooked,
insignificant in their size but they still held all
the beauty of mother nature's touch.
this gentle caress
that so easily breathed life
into nothing.
i liked the way they were always so underestimated.

   sometimes:
i think that in a way,
we loved each other with water in mind.
every 'i love you' sounded like violent rain on top of
the car when you're driving in a storm,
or how boiling water screams.
this intensity that gurgled deep inside me
until it spouted from my mouth uncontrollably,
at every chance it got.
it is strange though.
now that i live in drought,
i'd give anything to hear a cascade of affection leave
your mouth and flow towards me.

i am nothing if i am not my body

i am nothing if i am not my body.
i don't know how to exist as anything more.
and so i moan,
breath heavier,
tighten my legs around them.
this is what i am built for,
this is what everyone looks at me and imagines.
my body
is not mine most days,
i belong to whichever man has decided i am his.
i am on my knees, begging to not be,
i want to be more.
i want my body to be mine again.
i so miss how it used to belong to me.

our clocks

i was so ready for you,
i really was.
but i guess you just weren't.
we were just running with different clocks,
the times never quite lined up for us,
did they, love?

patience

i thought i'd found my person.
part of me still does,
to be honest.
i just can't quite believe that this is the end of us,
i don't know whether that's because i don't want to
or whether the universe is telling me
just to hold on,
just a little bit tighter
and with a little bit more

patience.

i never was any good at that, was i?
being patient.
but in my eyes, you were so damn right for me
there was no point in waiting.

i know this is the end right now, and i don't
know how long this end will last for
but i will never stop wondering when the next start
will begin.
there must be more to us,
to our story together.

an open letter to the first boy to broke my heart

i've been told that you never forget your first love,
and i agree.
but i have also been told that the second heartbreak
is so much worse than the first.
this i cannot agree with.

now, i haven't experienced this hypothetical
'second heartbreak' yet, but-
wholeheartedly-
i know it will pale in comparison to ours.

i think i will compare every future boy to you,
they probably won't hold me with the same hunger,
or kiss me with the same need,
or touch me with the same gentle passion.
in a way,
i don't think i'd be able to cope if they did,
i don't think i ever want anyone to touch me the way
you did.
that was ours,
those brushes of shoulders, fingers, lips,
ours.
they'll always be ours.

you know for a long time,
a really,
really long time,
i had thought it was us against
the world,
against everyone else.
i imagined us getting married,
and growing old together,
and living every second in between.

god,
i don't know if i will ever love anyone

the way i loved you,
with such an innocence
and with so much trust.

even writing this, i have that stupid voice in the back of
my head,
the one i block out, and refuse to listen to.
it is telling me that this was the right decision
but i sort of hate that you made it for me.
that voice sounds a lot like you nowadays,
the same breathless laugh,
or raises in pitch.
i'm really trying not to listen to it.

oh darling,
i wish i could say that a first heartbreak will be like you
are morning a loved one,
but it is so much worse.
at least death is final,
there is nothing final about still being in love with a
ghost,

and you are haunting me.

in my dreams

in my dreams,
you're still with me.
and so i find myself begging for sleep most evenings,
daytimes too,
just hoping that in some way,
i can experience us together again.
for just a little while.
when i wake,
when i am pulled away from you again,
i lay there and try to remember every word you said,
every light touch,
every precious moment.
it is the only way i can ever be with you now,
so i beg for sleep.

i was desperate for someone to realise

i don't think it was ever hard to see that
i was struggling.
i started smoking too much,
i was reckless,
i lost my passion for living,

i stopped quietly pleading for help, i was begging for it.

everything,

was
an absolute
cry
for help.

the truth

i was doing really well, i was.
i don't know what happened.
i felt like finally i had it all figured out, all in control.
that five year plan mapped out,
an x marking the spot to a future with you.

i had imagined it all,
day dreamed
about every single second we'd spend together.
the shared laughter
as we'd watch other couples
struggle to find what we had, what came so easily.
it practically fell into our laps.
babies with your eyes, but my nose,
your smile, but my teeth,
your brains, and my wits.

i so wanted them to look like you.
i wanted more of you in the world,
oh, i still do,
but god we fucked up somewhere along the way.

how am i supposed to do anything now?
i can't plan a future with anyone else,
all i'll see is you in their place and
i really think
i'd resent them for not being you.
i just wanted to grow old with you,
hold hands while walking not just for love,
but for support.
i don't want anyone the way i want you.
truthfully
i don't think i ever will.

i broke my own heart

you know i think i broke my own heart in a way.
i mean sure,
you placed every nail in the coffin,
you started the fire,
you ripped me apart piece by piece,
but i just watched you do it.
i begged for more of you,
and you agreed, knowing wholeheartedly
i would not be getting anymore.
and i think i always knew exactly that.
deep down,
i think my heart knew i would never get
any more from you.
i suppose love is a bit tainted for me now,
after ours.
spoilt with the idea that love will always be one person
besotted
while the other just sits and watches.
i think i will always be the one who loves
too hard,
too fast,
too much.
and so i broke my own heart,
didn't i?
because you never wanted me
in all of my vulnerability,
or my infatuation,
and yet i gave it anyway.
i'm so sorry, heart,
i really am so sorry.

salt water lips

i used to think if time travel was possible,
there was only one thing i would choose to do.
i didn't care
about reliving my favourite moments with friends,
all smiles
and sore sides from giggling too hard.
i didn't ever want to experience or
relish in our best memories either,
and i certainly didn't want to fix the bad ones.

i used to think all i would do was prevent myself
from meeting you.
i'd probably have ripped so many holes into
the fabric of space and time.
i'd help save myself from the love, and the eventual
heartbreak.
how selfless of me.

i think i know now that i wouldn't go back
and prevent our
crossing of paths.
if time travel was possible,
if it ever becomes possible,
i would go back to when you held me
in that cold,
english ocean,
and kissed me for the first time.
when you wrapped a towel around me on the beach,
and we watched the sun go down in between watching
each other.

i'd memorise every detail of your face again,
and taste
the salt water on your lips.
i'd feel the grit of sand on the back of your neck
and in your hair,

i'd hold you,
with a hunger and need you probably
wouldn't have understood.

i felt like i was finally home
when i was with you.
no one has ever made me feel like that before.

no one has since.

i could so easily do without it

most days i do wish i did not exist.

and not in the
'i am going to kill myself'
way,
'i want everyone to mourn me'
way,

but in the
'living just seems to be too much effort for me'
way.

i could so easily do without it.

always you

i'd pull out every single eyelash if it meant i got to wish
for you to come back to me.

every birthday candle that's blown out,
every dandelion i pick,
every star in that stupid fucking sky.

it's always you.
always.

but it's just never me,
is it, love?

how many girls

to the man
who recorded me during sex without
asking for my consent first.
when i looked up at you,
my eyes filled with nothing
but trust
and love,
did you even see the way you broke me?
the way my breathing
stopped,
and my hands
shook.
i was 18, i was so young.
you have no idea
of the damage you caused me that day.

and to the man
who didn't listen when i said no.
who told me that he thought i was 'just kidding,'
and that if he 'kept trying,'
eventually i'd stop saying no and start
moaning for him.
you told me
you'd always look after me.
you broke up with me 20 minutes later, left me asleep
in a puddle of my own tears
and i've never been able to have sex properly since.

and to the man
i considered a close friend, but considered me
just an easy hookup to brag about.
who allowed strangers to tell me they heard all about
how my body looks naked,
how i was easy enough that
if they just asked
nicely,

maybe they could see it too.
human beings are not sex toys.
i am not your sex toy.

i have so many ghosts,
i cannot have sex in peace anymore.
i can't have sex without crying,
or without feeling my heart drop.
i am haunted by these
fucking
men.
these men that want my warmth,
my legs wrapped around them,
my mouth silent for all sounds except whimpers.
this is all i will ever be good for,
this is all they will ever want from me.

my sexual trauma,
is not what i wanted to ever write about
but most days i cannot wake up
without tasting it in the back of my throat.
how many girls-
how many young, teenage girls
have gone through what i have gone through?
i ache for us.
i ache for us.

self stitched

we were supposed to be
each other's.
it was us,
we were meant to be us.
but you tore yourself away from me.
and i bled.
i had to stitch myself back together without you.
and it was agonising,
devastating, it really was,
and so fucking painful.
and every night, every dream i had of you
made those stitches unravel,
wounds opening up,
my blood stained everything i touched.
every time i saw your name on my phone,
or hear a laugh that sounded like yours,
see a boy with hair like yours,
i'd feel part of me break again.
it doesn't feel like this is ever going to end.

come back

i still miss you. a
lot some days, less on

others, but you are always
in the back of my

mind. it is excruciating, honestly,
it is ruining me. it's

been months now, and
i think about you a hell

of a lot less. i
haven't cried in a long

time. but as much as
i like to say that

i'm healed, there's a tiny
part of me i can't

fix. and it's the part
you broke. but you know

the worst thing? the worst
bit of it all, is

i'd probably open my arms
as wide as they were

the last time i saw
you, if you ever decided

to come back to me.

i don't want to write about him anymore

i don't want to still be so in love with him,
so besotted.
i don't want to hover over our chats, typing out
half a message.
i don't want any of this,
because i know all i'm doing is hurting him.
even after everything,
after the hurt he caused me,
the pain
and the love
and the tsunami of tears,
i just don't want to break him any more than we both
already are.

i don't want to break him the way he broke me.

distanced

in our time apart,
i found myself longing to dream of you.
a sort of compromise to the distance,
i think.
i'd lay there, imagining a thousand different scenarios,
begging my brain to latch onto one idea and run with it.
i swear,
i probably would've made a deal with the devil
if it had meant
that i got to touch your lips with mine
just one more time,
awake or not.

and when i wasn't falling asleep to memories of you,
i was waking up to a half empty bed,
with a half empty heart.
an even emptier day, without you there to help fill it.
i know, i know,
in a relationship you should to be your own person,
you shouldn't become dependent,
but if the sun did not exist, what would the moon do
with all of their spare time?

what am i meant to do when i can't tell you how shitty
my days been?
or when a new song i hear reminds me of you?
or when my heart is aching from missing you?

i read once,
that the strings in your heart can sometimes break
because of some deep emotional trauma.
something about making your heart lose shape,
blood can't pump properly and often it ends in dying.
it's fucking crazy how powerful love is,
like it can literally kill you while simultaneously being
one of the only reasons to stay alive.

i think maybe that's why i feel like
i'm being ripped in two.

this distance never gets easier,
practice definitely does not make perfect.
its like an open wound you never let heal,
constantly pulling the skin apart,
picking at scabs,
sprinkling salt in for good measure.
i turned myself inside out loving you,
as you did for me.
and tonight,
i'll fall asleep cocooned in my duvet,
imagining that you're willing yourself to have dreams
of me,
as i am of you.

girls like us

for girls like us, love can never be anything other than
a boy salivating over our naked bodies.
we moan for someone else's pleasure, not ours.
you are there to cheer them up, to turn them on, to
throw your head back and look pretty.
it is heartbreaking.
it is shattering.
what a stupid girl,
begging for anything else.
i've already told you,
girls like us do not get anything else.

today

today,
was not a good day.
today was bad.
i was consumed with thoughts
that were nothing
but unkind.

this depression,
it grabbed onto me,
attached itself like a ball and chain
i was a prisoner to
myself,
to my mind.

and i wallowed,
i self pitied.
i did everything
i hate,
i showed
no compassion
i wrote poem after
poem on how
i hate me.
i wrote about him again, after i promised myself
i wouldn't.

i didn't eat,
i smoked near a whole pack of cigarettes
and i held myself.

my arms felt like barbed wire.

i have become the girl

i have become the girl known for heartbreak
because, truthfully,
there is not a single ounce in my body
that is not
always ready to love somebody.
i am built upon the chance of romance occurring,
prayers, and kisses, and sunflowers.
i-
i am a cyclic book that can be read over and over
and each time,
the heartbreak gets a little bit worse
and a little bit more painful.
and each time it ends with me, alone
begging not to be.
i am begging
not to be.

completion is so sought after

i miss feeling complete.
like i've got my shit together,

and it really is the little things.
looking up at the moon at night,
waking up and opening my curtains without scowling,
taking pictures of my friends when they're laughing.
i miss putting on perfume
and
finishing books
and
eating a meal without feeling guilty.
i miss kissing someone
because i love them
instead of
just because i'm drunk
and a stranger wants to take me home.
i miss having fun sober,
i miss going to bed before the sun comes up,
i miss listening to music that makes me want to sing
along badly.

i think i'm an absolute mess most days.
i have no more energy for living
i feel like i'm just barely existing
and i hate it.
it is such an empty way of experiencing the world.

the idea of you

maybe i did just love the idea of you.
but god,
it was such
a good idea.

excuses

i am so sick of excuses.
of men giving me half of them
and expecting my contentment.
i am sick of the 'you're too good for me' drivel
which really
is just another way of saying
'i've stopped trying'
i'm too good for you?
so be better, do more.
i have never begged for anything above the
bare minimum
and yet somehow,
i'm still just asking for too much.
a 'get home safe' text,
a surprise date,
a bunch of fucking flowers,
a little love note left for me to find,
a call on your way home from work,
an 'i love you' said not just instead of 'goodbye',
but with meaning and passion, and actions not words.
i mean, fuck
do you even know how many different ways
you can say 'i love you'?
i just want someone,
for once,
to say it
and fucking mean it.
i really want someone to mean it.

the one after you

i really did feel so guilty the other day.
he held me and kissed me on my forehead.
i think it was the first time i felt my heart beat since
you'd stopped it.
because i mean,
that is what you did.
it's cliche to say it,
but fuck,
you let me take my own heart out of my chest to give to
you,
and then,
you just

dropped
it.

and yeah, when he picked it up the other day,
oh,
i felt so guilty.
when he touched my body in a way you never did,
with this gentle caress that told me he understood.
i didn't even have to explain
anything.

aftermath

and it is only now i realise how differently
we handled our break up.
while you replaced my body with someone else's,
i tried to replicate what we had.
you wrapped yourself around another person,
i collected every part of you i still had and stuck it to
someone else.
i fell in love in the hope it would make me fall out of
love with you.

it didn't.

and while i cried and
held myself,
you didn't shed a single tear.
i was so desperate for us to come back together
you couldn't have cared less.

you just wanted another pair of legs to be between,
i wanted nothing to be between us.

i learnt to live without you

and i didn't have anyone to stare at the moon with.
so i stared at it by myself,
and i remembered how it felt have you there with me.

and i didn't have anyone to buy me
sunflowers anymore.
so i bought them for myself
and i couldn't help but remember how pretty the ones
you used to buy me were.

and i didn't have anyone to hold me.
so i learnt to hold myself,
but my arms never quite feel as comforting
as yours did.

and i didn't have anyone to love me.
so i tried to love myself.
i can't do this one yet,
not yet.

sunflowers

and if there was ever a way to describe
the personal defeat of realising
that i no longer held the happiness i once did,

i would tell you about the day i found out that
sunflowers
do not in fact face each other when there is no sun.

instead,
the bend at their neck
and droop their heads towards the ground.

you always did wonder why i like sunflowers so much.

the broken you

they will never understand the pain they caused you.
how it felt to have your heart ripped out and
trodden on,
one heavy footed stamp for each betrayal.
they didn't have to feel it like you did,
my love.
and so i won't sit here preaching some self help bullshit
about it making you stronger,

but i will say this:

withstanding a beating like that means your soul
will blossom with
blue and black bruises,
scars that look like
slivers of silver will
adorn your mind,
and that tiny part of you that remained whole
will forever remember
what it was like for the rest of you to match.

fuck them,
the 'broken' you is so much more enticing,
and they will never have the privilege of meeting it.

and one day

and one day,
one day you'll be showering,
and you'll use up the very bit
of that body wash of yours that
he liked.

or one day your song will come on in the car,
and it wont be
until the end
that you remember how he looked at you
as he sung it.
you might not even picture his face anymore.

one day that coat he gave you
stops being that coat that he gave you
and is just a coat.

it is sad that memories fade, and that love fades
but one day,
you'll see the beauty in it.
they wont always be the first thing
you think about every morning
or the last thing before you brains drift into sleep,
or the thing you dream about.

moving on will take time,
but one day,
you'll realise you feel different,
and it's because you don't love them anymore.

the list

and like most girls,
if you go into my phone,
deep into my notes folder
you'll find
'the list'.
and like most girls i have this thing organised,
categorically entered based on dates,
detailed events,
ratings of how they kissed me,
how they touched me.

i mean these lists are thorough,
extensive.
full names,
alongside comments they made about my body,
which parts they deemed touchable,
which fake whimper they liked best.

most girls have these lists, this is normal nowadays.
this is how we rate human interaction in
its most vulnerable state.

my sexual assaults are on this list.
they sour it for me.
give me a small pang in my chest,
they make my mouth run dry.

believe me i have tried to erase them.
i cannot fall asleep without reliving them,
i cannot dream of anything but them.
the fact that i am even having to use a plural here
makes me wince unbelievably.
a list of sex and sexual assaults all merged into one,

but,
i look at it this way,

i have placed these men in this application,
i have given them descriptions,
and extensive explanations.
they belong to a single day.
granted,
on that day,
i may have also belonged to them,
but no more.

i will heal,
i will record my experiences,
i will move on.
this is beyond just me,
this is for every women who has a list,
for every women who was not taught
consensual encounters from
non-consensual ones,
for every women listening to this
with her heart
in her mouth
and her chest
empty,
you are so much more than what has happened to your
body.
so much more.

our lists do not define us,
the length
is no ones business but our own.
the contents
belong to us and no one else.
i am so sorry if you have ever been told otherwise.

and for those of you with lists similar to myself,
that have rotting carcasses of you
buried in between fresh bodies,
know that you are not as tainted as you think.
they have tried to pollute you

but i will do everything i can to
breath life back into you.

i will leave you with this.
there will come a day where this list
is nothing but a collection of names.
you will no longer be owned by them,
and the list is exactly that,

just a list.

my almost

if someone were to ask me about you,
i don't think i would know what to say.
i don't feel sad when I hear your name anymore,
so,
that's progress right?

don't get me wrong,
i feel something,
i just can't quite put my finger on what it is yet.
i hope one day, to feel peace.
i hope one day,
not hear your name anymore.

and i can't quite seem to help feeling slightly
pathetic at times.
i mean,
technically, i was nothing to you.
it didn't matter that we'd stay chatting on swing sets
till the day turned into the next,
or that you told me you liked me more than you'd ever
liked anyone else,
you still hurt me.
you still lied.

i think what's worse,
is you did it with such cut throat ruthlessness,
holding the heart i gave you
in one hand,
and hers
in your other.
i've never quite known someone
to be so quick to fall for me,
and to take half of that time to drop me.

i do not wish to be misconstrued when
i say that i have moved on.

this does not mean you are no longer accountable for
the pain that you caused me,
it is just to say,
i know i deserved more.
he,
gives me more.
he does not give me the broken promises,
the inconsistencies,
the unknowing.
he does not hold anyone's heart in his hands
but mine.

in some strange way,
i am thankful that you were my almost.
i am thankful for two reasons:

1. you gave me my first experience with heart-
    break. i know how deeply my heart can feel
    now, and i am prepared for the next time it is
    squeezed too tightly by someone i let hold it.

2. if you had not been my almost, i would not
    have met my complete. for this, i can almost
    forgive you for everything. because trust me,
    he is so worth the hurt.

happiness

i think,
truly,
this might be the first time
that i've felt like i've belonged.
like i have a place in this world and,
for once,
i am so sure that
not only do i fit perfectly,
but the world fits me too.

and i don't feel empty anymore,
i have no pieces begging to be found.
no missing emotions,
or numb moments.

i am no longer questioning whether i am
half full
or half empty

this feeling, this complete satisfaction is something
i have chased for so long.
i have begged
and pleaded
in silent cries of prayer to anyone who would listen.
someone,
must
have been listening.

believe me,
deep down i know this feeling may not last forever,
but i think this makes me treasure it more.
i am treating my happiness with great fragility
and i will not let anyone hold it
but me.

missed opportunity

you get one go in this world,
one.
measly.
go.

one.

there are no do overs,
no repeats,
no second chances.
and when you do look back at
every missed opportunity,
every time you said no,
i can promise you,
you will feel nothing but regret.

that 'what if' will never leave your lips but your mind
will whisper it forever.
you should've told that person how you felt,
said yes to every crazy, last minute plan,
experienced the world in every light possible.

you should live every day
like tomorrow is never coming,
like yesterday was your best day yet and
like today has the chance to be even better.

you should embrace every rejection,
every emotion,
every new person who enters your life,
because there is nothing wrong
with negative experiences,
at least this means you gave it your all.

trust me,
your life will fill others with a beautiful technicolor.

you can do so much for this world,
so much good.

so do not fear the unknown,
or the sadness,
there is no guardian angel that is going to protect you
from yourself.
there is only missed opportunity,

and you do not want to miss a second of this.

effortlessly

with time you begin to learn that
the best way to live life is
effortlessly.
that to sit and watch the universe take control is
so much more satisfying
than to try to fight against it.

because water can so easily become the tea
that you drink when the warmth
is the only thing that will stop your hands from shaking.

you can turn seeds into flowers,
and experience growth from situations you would
have never thought possible.
you can bloom again,
i promise you, darling.
and you will,
effortlessly.

unbelievably happy

and when i look back at one of the hardest moments
of my life so far,
when i gave my everything to someone who really,
didn't deserve
even a slither of me,
i'm sort of filled with this warmth.

and it is so strange,
to find happiness in being hurt,
but i remember how my best friend held me,
and brought me tissues, and chocolate,
and listened to me cry for months.

i remember how it felt
to wake up for the first time
and not need to
wash the salt off of my cheeks.

i remember how it felt
to write about being happy again,
and not about how you broke my heart.

there is so much growth
a person can do when they are hurt
in the way i was.
and when i look back at just how much i have grown in
these last few months,
it makes me
so
unbelievably happy.

i just cant wait
to see what the next few months hold for me.

dancing around the sun

today,
i have turned 20 years old.
that means i have revolved around this sun
20 times already,

i have done that.

now, granted
i had the help of the earth,
the people who kept me on it,
the people who loved me
when i held no loved for myself,
but i lived long enough for my 20th waltz
with this beautiful sun.

and as she spun me around her,
my feet moving too fast for my own body,
the only thought trickling through my mind was how
fun it is to dance again.
and how i will try to always remember that this dance
never needs to end.

the sun and i,
will have our arms outstretched to one another
no matter the time of day.
and even when i cannot see anything but her absence,
she will forever let me blindly pirouette
and encircle her.
with about as much grace as a newborn calf,
trembling,
all knock kneed
and greedy mouthed.
she knows i struggle to find my own footing most days,
but she dances with me anyway.

and so on the day i finished my 20th twirl with the sun,

i made two promises to myself.

1

on days where i do not want to be alive anymore,
i promise myself i will look up
towards my never-ending dance partner.
i will bask in her warmth
and i will let her dry the tears on my face
into streaks of salt
that will season my heart with recovery and growth.

2

i promise myself that i will make it to my 21st rotation
around the sun,
and i will thank her
for dancing with me always.

acknowledgements

this will be cheesy, i will cry as i write this and i can promise you i will add someone new into this last page every single day before i finally send the book into the world for you to read.

there are so many people who have helped me become the person i am now proud to be; a lot of them are mentioned in between the lines of my poems, but they deserve so much more than that.

so,

thank you to the boy who broke my heart, for showing me how deeply i can love, but also how explosive heartache can be. you joked once that i should thank you for hurting me, for giving me 'more poetry content'. thank you, and fuck you, but mainly thank you. i grew from the pain in a way i didn't think people could. starved of sunlight, i still bloomed.

thank you to the amazing women who raised me. she single handedly watered me, placed me in the sun and allowed me to flourish. i owe you everything.

thank you to the two people who showed me what love can look like. your relationship is what most people dream of, i know i do. truthfully, i would love to refer to our friendship as life changing but, wholeheartedly, i know it is so much more than just friendship. i have found parts of you in me, and parts of me in you. you educate me, you ground me, you are the cheerleaders in my corner always.

thank you to the girl who has truly acted like my sister for the last 5 years. you have been by my side throughout every difficulty, as teenage life often is full of. even when you're stealing my clothes, or begging me to pick you up on the other side of town, you are the most annoying and lovable person i have ever met. no matter what, i will always love you, with every part of my heart.

thank you to my dearest friends. i would write pages dedicated to each of you, the majority of this book is exactly that. i adore each and every one of you and you teach me every day how to be a better person, with kindness and so much compassion. i would not be here without you. i will do everything i can to make sure you bloom, the next time you are covered in moonlight.

thank you to the many people who taught me to love again, who taught me i can experience a different, healthier love and it can be just as good as the toxic shit.

thank you to anyone who has ever listened to or read my poetry. to anyone who has followed my journey on social media and has now followed my journey through this book. your support means the absolute world to me. without it, i would still be a girl, writing shitty poetry in her room, too scared to let anyone read it. i've never mentioned this to you, but before posting my very first video on tiktok, only 3 people had ever heard my poetry. within a couple of hours, hundreds of thousands of you had. it was simultaneously the scariest and best thing i have ever done.

our journey is not over. no, in fact, it is far from that. to the next poem, the next chapter, the next heartbreak, the next fall, the next bloom under moonlight.

thank you, for everything.

a few pages for your poetry

ah, so you made it to the end then, my darling.

the next few pages are blank, on purpose, don't worry.

i want you to fill them with your own words, with
drawings, with thoughts, with poetry. write for yourself,
for no one else. you do not have to show anyone.

this is for you.

these words are yours.

.

153

thank you :)

Made in the USA
Coppell, TX
21 December 2023

26735742R00085